EASTERN STAR

Eastern Star

A collection of poems
by
DAVID DEPHY

Adelaide Books
New York / Lisbon
2020

EASTERN STAR
A collection of poems
By David Dephy

Copyright © by David Dephy
Cover design © 2020 Adelaide Books
Cover Art by David Dephy, Brooklyn, New York, 2018

Published by Adelaide Books, New York / Lisbon
adelaidebooks.org

Editor-in-Chief
Stevan V. Nikolic

All rights reserved. No part of this book may be reproduced in any manner whatsoever without written permission from the author except in the case of brief quotations embodied in critical articles and reviews.

For any information, please address Adelaide Books
at info@adelaidebooks.org
or write to:
Adelaide Books
244 Fifth Ave. Suite D27
New York, NY, 10001

ISBN: 978-1-953510-65-5

Printed in the United States of America

For my wife Kethy

Contents

The Path into the Dark Is Golden *11*

The Sea Is So Calm Now *12*

In Front of the Mirror *13*

Politics Is the Art of Choices *14*

Poethree D *16*

Eastern Star *18*

If a Life Means the Breath *20*

The Drift of Understanding *21*

People *23*

Walking on the Street *25*

The Interpretation *27*

The Apex of the Discipline *29*

The Drift of Context *31*

Yes, I Love You More Than I Love Angels *34*

Night Above the Forest *35*

I Opened Myself Today *39*

The Poewer of Poetry Perfected *41*

Should I Say *44*

You Yourself *45*

You Are the Center *47*

You Are Light *49*

To Be Written *52*

The World Opens Before Me *54*

West *55*

The Way Home *57*

Shared Lane *59*

The Same Ode to distant friend *61*

The Light of Wish *63*

The Art of E-Art-H *64*

Something Is Important *66*

Put Yourself in My Place, Ghost *67*

Poetryoga *69*

I Hear a Speech, My Love *70*

I Release You, Go With Peace *72*

I'd like to Explain *73*

I Transformed *74*

If I Can Find You Someone Else Will Find You Too *77*

Naked *79*

Our Love Is the Promise *80*

Please Accept *81*

For the Sake of Love *83*

How Can I *85*

Don't Wait *87*

Deep in the Heart of Heaven *90*

I See Your Smile *91*

Lord's Verses *92*

Oh Lord I See with My Beating Heart *93*

Bear Word to the Spartans *95*

When I Go Out *96*

The Fireflies *97*

Every New Second *98*

Acknowledgement *99*

About the Author *101*

The Path into the Dark Is Golden

The path into the dark is golden.
I am moving forward to reach the
point. My shadow is floating behind
me as the answer of a secret which
had been stolen and we are hungry for
light and still we are going,
despite everything, despite the rules —
despite the laws of the universe speechless,
you spurred yourself into life… Because,
besides you I am not searching anything in you.

March 14, 2019

The Sea Is So Calm Now

"You are free now from all your fears," the wave
says, playing around my feet. "And yes, now you
know why a calm sea does not make a skilled sailor."

Every time I see the calm sea
I remember voices from my childhood,
I look for a word that was never spoken.

The sea is calm, like the face of a child after dark night's
unrest. I love its breathing, the movement of waves, like a
mother's breath, is so loving that in the past they

put out the alarm, the storm, the fears of childhood
and now calm some future alarm and fears and storm
off the whole world's coast. Yes, that was the moment I found

a word that had been spoken only once, maybe, or was never
spoken at all. All these storms are in me now, that's
why I'm calm, I am the captain of all calmness, mother.

February 27, 2019

In Front of the Mirror

I am standing in front of the mirror, the reflection
of myself is asking me: "Would life be better if we
could forget the past? Would life be better if we could
forget the present? Forget this very second when
we are trying to stay alive here — in this multi-language
labyrinth of our wishes called New York City?" I feel
joy is dawning in me, I feel peace is near and
guess right away — I am dreaming myself.

Am I dying into the void? I don't think so. I don't
know. But I can feel the flow of memories. I can hear.
It has a gold-color body — I am hearing it's crystal voice,
the breeze is singing for me: "The memories always
tells us what is right and what's not, memories are the
winds, all kinds of memories, beautiful or ugly make life
worth living and make death impossible." Yet I
guess right away — I am dreaming myself.

February 21, 2019

Politics Is the Art of Choices

I see the tear-drop,
the drop of blood,
the drop of sweat
on my palm,
the aircraft still
flying up above,
the sounds of the bombs –
of the falling, falling,
falling bombs are chasing
deafness of an epoch,
they are going through
my wishes and this smoke,
this black smoke above our hope
is covering heaven –
full of drops that from our blood
we throw for the future to drink,
which may steal below to quench
the hunger of knowing in some
spirit in some shadow there
hidden – far beneath, under all
scripts, far beneath and long ago,
far beneath the memories' waves
and far beneath the breath of us,
we can feel the reason of all the

tear-drops so fatefully desired –
the politics like knowing things
throughout peace-time before
or after or during the war, is the
art of the choice, the art of the law,
of mankind's solitude at all.

April 7, 2019

Poethree D

Through the rays of the night I can speak out, speak to
myself boldly and loudly about all my doubts, beliefs
or fears, about all my emotions, memories and love.

I am on the ground. I am sitting in front of the bonfire.
I am feeling the calmness of air and breathing deeply
with my whole body. The rain is about to start. I am not

alone here, I am with these elements of silence. "Divine,"
I am saying this one word and the fire is answering me:
"It's the nature of freedom." "Devotion," I am saying this

one word and the earth is answering me: "There are no rules
to follow and no litmus tests to measure your responsibility."
"Doing," I am saying this one word and air is answering:

"Doing means staying alive and this is the sense of
responsibility." "Day," I am saying this one word to the
drop on my palm and this trembling drop of the rain is

answering me: "You stand responsibility by declaration.
The stand for responsibility validates and reinforces itself."
I am remembering the smile, that divine smile of that child

who saw his father after war and sitting on the ground in front of a bonfire under the starting rain and breathing silence of night, that child's smile makes me human.

January 24, 2019

Eastern Star

If there is no freedom within you, you won't inspire anyone.
If a star is born only in the sky and not
in you, you won't see the light.
If heaven is not in you, you will never get there.
If there is hell in you, you will never escape from there.

If you are not forgiving, you will never breathe freely.
If you don't give, you will never fly.
If you lose hope, you will never wake up.
If you don't steer your passion,
you will never quench your yearning

You told me one day — I am your song.
Your breath is the song and the song is like me.
Children are playing - soon calmness will come.
I feel your breath in front of the gate

So far, so far, so near and so far…

You're the vineyard's gate and this gate is the heart.
The heart is the choice, the choice is the way.
You are what I think and always you are.
You are what I saw and always you were

So far, so far, so near and so far…

So, let me sing in your transparent breath.
Be like the wine in your divine veins.
I am wishing to let you hear the song - as I am
and let me please you — you know I need this too

So far, so far, so near and so far…

All the words' variations come down to one truth.
And all the ideas come down to one breath.
And all the world's secrets in your heart are revealed.
Till the star of the East is the sign of the future

So near and not far… Almighty and calm…

Eastern star is trembling all over me
and also all over you — we hear and we see
the spirit of silence within our breathe.
Oh yes, one which we take and yes, one which we leave.

May 8, 2018

If a Life Means the Breath

If a life means the breath,
then the breath means a way.

So, here we are —
and we are still going,
we are still rushing,
we are still the same.

So, this is life
as we know it,
with a great distance
between now and then,

between a tree and its
shadow, between a thirst
and water, between
a cold and fire,

between a fall and the
ground, between a suffocation
and air. Distance means
senselessness when your

loved one means the
meaning of life.

August 6, 2019

The Drift of Understanding

For the one real closest person
is the one who knows your past,
is the one who believes in your

future and accepts you as you
are now. Understanding is a
message that equals a loaded gun.

Look at this familiar shadows
in the afternoon. Look at this
familiar night and its fireflies,

they are the jewels wrecked
by the darkness. Look at this familiar,
example of how the commitment,

yes the commitment
is different from wants,
is different from intention,
is different from your needs,
there is the beauty of intervening,
when you find yourself in your own wishes,
when you find yourself in the others' wishes too,
when you find yourself on your own way,

when you find yourself like that firefly in
heart of darkness, so you take
action that directs you toward the
accomplishment of your goal.

It requires you shift your behavior now
in the face of drift, our life is drift
of understanding, in between the shores'
of choices, sometimes noisy sometimes

noiseless, the world with it always rejoices
while we can see ourselves in each other's
silence, while the one real nearest person
remains the one who recognizes your smile.

December 14, 2018

People

You love people — that's great.
People love you — that's great.
"We, the people" — that's really
great. We are breathe of
universe... Oh wait... Wait, wait
and... Listen:

People —
The shadows' collective of hope.
People —
The meaning of God's synthetic
personality.
People —
The meaning of devilish emptiness.
People —
The edge between the freedom and
the illusions. You are alone or you're

with them, you're loving with them,
praying or living, you have to choose
between these feelings, between these
words, between these cases and you will
do that, like the ray embraces around the

nakedness of darkness. And the question
remains the same — Is the finish line the
starting line? You have to choose and
you will do that, yet the question remains
the same — wait, and the answers will

surprise you — People show you what they
can become, when they need you.

December 9, 2018

Walking on the Street

I am walking on the street and the echoes
of my footsteps are telling me: "You can buy
a luxury watch or just a watch but every
watch in the world is telling the time, not
the truth."

I am walking on the street and the echoes
of my footsteps are telling me: "You can buy
a luxury suit or just a suit, but every suit
in the world is telling the fashion, not your
nakedness."

I am walking on the street and the echoes
of my footsteps are telling me: "You can buy
a luxury house or just a house, but every
house in the world is showing the place, not
your home."

And the smile on faces and the sadness
on faces, or the happiness on faces,
or the fear on faces is telling me: "Your
home, your nakedness and the truth are only

in your loved one's heart and the only real
way to the only real richness in the only

real world without any illusions around,
are going only through your loved one's heart.

Your breath is going across your loved one's
heart-beats." I am walking on the street,
I am hearing what the faces say and I know
what time it is now, I know how I am naked
now, I am breathing for you now — I know

the truth.

December 10, 2018

The Interpretation

I am holding out a handful of water. There are endless
rivers deep within my handful of water. I see my smile there,
I hear the voice from deep within: "You can only interpret
yourself given the state of affairs you
were thrown into at birth.
Your birth is your interpretation of your future."

I am holding out a handful of sand. There are the endless
mountains deep within my handful of sand. I see my shadow
on it, I hear the voice from deep within: "You cannot change
the facts, but you can shift the importance of the facts in how
you interpret them."

I am holding out a handful of breath. There are endless
winds deep within my handful of breath. It's trembling, I see
myself through this breath and I am hearing the voice:
"The facts of your history and belief, discover the possible
interpretations available to you,

while you cannot change the facts of your history and belief,
you can shift your interpretation of those facts. Everything is
intimately connected with your personal interpretations."
I am holding out a handful of ashes, I burned all my sorrows
with my breath and then

this ash became silence, silence became
the presentiment of joy and the joy became the
water again on my palms. I am holding out a handful of
words. There is the life-giving force in my handful of words,
these words are endless Interpretations

of myself, of my spirit, of all my wishes. I try to tell you
through the language of interpretation how strange
the world is, but I hear the voice: "You think your
language was invented to describe and represent
reality, but language,

reality and all your wishes are intertwined — language
not only shapes our interpretation of reality, but shapes
how the reality itself unfolds." Let me unfold you my love,
while the language of silence is covering
us, while the language
of your beauty is speaking in me.

December 11, 2018

The Apex of the Discipline

Sometimes it's hard to understand
what's going on in your heart, you
feel as you are homeless, you
feel some transformation, but
transformation requires not surely
that you understand, but that you trust.

The trust is the heart of prescience
and it's as a duty – an end state in the
future that governs your step in the present.
Your dedicate yourself to your goal, yeah
sometimes it's hard to predict is it
growing into something more?

Sometimes it's hard to realize
but always easy to feel the meaning
of this dedication — the meaning
isn't thing or action, but sign of your
identity, where the identity is as breath,
breathe in breathe out — that's a gift no doubt,

it requires you to discipline yourself to think,
to feel, your presentiment as what's
demonstrated in your thoughts, in your

wishes and your words, and your actions,
for sure. There's the link between the
people, your tender-lovers and your foes.

As you begin to see that you are your own
manifestation in your words, must the show
go on? Yeah it must. Life is long or even short
we want to find a time which is lost, it gets
harder toward the apex, climb always toward
the apex, your summit is your home.

December 12, 2018

The Drift of Context

There is a context — an invisible environment,
the interrelated conditions, the structure of
interpretation in which our life happens.
Life for me is a stream of whispers.

There is a context of our life and it is like air to a bird,
like water to a fish. The fish doesn't see water,
it isn't necessarily aware of water.
Life for me is a stream of shouts.

The same is with a bird and air.
And yet, everything in a fish's world is consistent
with and generated from the fact that fish exist in water.
Life for me is a stream of intention.

Similarly everything that shows up in our life,
every word we speak and every action we take is naturally
consistent with and indicative of our context.
Life for me is a stream of desire where context

is the way. Push yourself from where you are
where you want to be. Yes, the context is the
way to see where you are, while you're breathing.
Life for me is a stream of aspiration,

where you want to be headed, and where
you are going to end up given the direction
you are heading now and living somehow.
Life for me is a stream of endurance.

We assert that if we are committed to living
as though our life actually depends on it,
we will be fulfilled. The context is like drift.
Life for me is a stream of sympathy,

where the drift is the cultural result of our liking
to stay alive and this is the shift, that which is
already happening and from which the future
can be predicted with a fair degree of precision.

Life for me is a stream of secrets and joy.
Where its drift denotes the path of least resistance.
Life for me is a stream of inconceivable passion
of our cultural norms, our personal histories

and our shared culture both shape and are shaped
by the drift. The godhead of rushing river that sweeps us
along through our lives, predisposing us to act like
anyone else. The drift has no sides, it isn't good or bad,

it's just the current in which we float through life.
The learning to stay alive with the drift is in

human nature. Who is who, the host or stranger.
Life for me is a stream of childhood fears.

The reasons, the results, the fish, the birds,
all of us have mastered elucidation and
justification because of our need to be right.
Life for me is a stream of childhood miracles.

Our need to cover up the consequences of our
actions feels like our mother's voice. It is automatic
for us to give the reasons and explanations in all situations.
Reasons, in a sense, have us… Yes… Have us…

November 15, 2018

Yes, I Love You More Than I Love Angels

Yes, I love you more than I love angels
Heaven, I'm sorry, but that is the fact.

Yes, I love you like I love myself.
Homeland, I'm sorry, but this is the fact.

Yes, I love you, and I can't explain this,
how did I perceive you the way you are.

I drag myself towards waking,
but — dear heart! — The reality is just like
sanctity,

I open my eyes and see you again,
my mind fills up with you, just like
the silence is filling up its body
with music and now that time

really belongs to me, if I could see it,
in the present, in the future, if it ever comes.
If my love for you returns me to myself
again.

January 6, 2013

Night Above the Forest

Who knows? Yeah, who knows what is death?
Who knows what it means? Is it the greatest
loss in life? Maybe that tree thinks about us
who knows? Maybe the greatest loss is what dies

inside us while we are alive, while we try to stay alive.
There are great seconds in our life, the day we are
born, the day we realized we are here and the day
we can see why… And why we are alive,

with thoughts, words, with breath, opinions,
with a touch of the hand, a touch of the heart,
I'll be your bridge, your temple, through
a hazelnut-bush cluster I enter a path,

forest-lured, sky-lured and I'm in a coma
breathing oxygen with a fever
for you—
what caused my hunger? What made me

thirst for you? I dream of a forest, a silent forest,
where night floats above the branches,
my fears held in shadows, I knit around you,
I fit you in to me, spent, I spend for you

gold, I immeasurably measure you just
like silver—
I am stuck in a downpour, falling on me
and myself a rain of thoughts, words, breath,

of caresses, with the heart's judgment,
I follow material passions with my spirit,
I'll be your bridge, your temple,
I am in a coma, approaching you,

my thoughts mixed up, I can express myself
and at last through a word symphony
the sun has gladly reached me, morning light
I love the morning, I'll dawn you,

I'll illuminate you and exit the forest,
I'll exit you too, I'm a citizen of this world.
It is said, before the moment of death
there is a second when we are given signs,

and with these signs I guess everything,
see everything, and with seeds—syllables,
drop by drop I fall to pieces, I undress myself as if
I'm dressed in a shirt and three-fourths

of the universe, too, and from the window
the colors appear, the sound appears

like after the rain when I hover above the dew
with the sacred aroma of strange footsteps,

just like a dream, just as in childhood
the truth of joy and fear have vanished,
the thirst becoming real, and now, between
these realities and somewhere far, far away,

or closer still it seems to me
I am at war, the night giving birth to stars,
the morning approaching, by the faces of the poor
I'm left a wealthy men on shore where I made peace

beyond the shore my spirit ascending
and setting its course, existing, with the signs,
exiting with the light, exiting for resurrection,
when I fall to pieces, heaven too falls to pieces,

the forest resting upon rays of light,
giving birth to men, to angels,
to a chorus of virgins and I won't leave you alone
but I'll tell you something with a familiar voice,

for hope's sake—
it is said in the second, at the moment of death,
signs are given, all variety of signs, that I count
without end, how the four and three relates to

the perfect seven of the universe,
now, in front of you I am falling into three pieces,
from Earth to other earths, the clouds of other skies
that calm of the Pacific flow gives me pleasure.

I believe now that the Light makes this
world's light only shadows, and
those already there wish to enjoy
the aroma of violets and the love given to me
as a gift—

this makes me happy in advance,
this joy that is drifting to God,
eternity, and incomprehensible
mystery.

Who knows? Yeah, who knows what is death?
Who knows what it means? Is it the greatest
loss in life? Maybe that tree thinks about us
who knows? Maybe the greatest loss is what dies

inside us while we are alive, while we try to stay alive.
There are great seconds in our life, the day we are
born, the day we realized we are here and the day
we understand why and why we are alive.

November 6, 2018

I Opened Myself Today

I opened myself today,
opened myself and waited.

There's a rule and we know it.
"Those who know do not say
those who say do not know."
This rule determines who enters
your heart, but you decide
who stays. We try to appear
to be free, we try to smile
when we leave,

Yes, we know the rules,
we try to stay alive in this path
in between the choices, something
is gone, but something advanced,
our decision is our truth
and maybe it hurts, but it hurts
only once, but a lie always hurts
when we remember it and the stars

In our blood and in our sweat,
or even eyes, in our eyes,
in our thought in our bones

look so adorable like childhood's
smile, there are faces we love or we hate
though some remain and some
have gone and I opened myself so widely today,
I opened myself, I am waiting so long.

We entered the noise of the millennium,
a thousand years running through our veins
yes, I opened myself and waited,
I entered the breath of my loved one,
I am on my way in between choices,
this path is so strange and strongly unbroken,
my calmness waiting is getting so noisy
I keep myself wide open.

I am listening now, there is the flow,
the lilac flow of all our breathe
this flow told me word for word:

"There's a magic crown beneath which all is life.
Maybe we have to think or even always knew.
Who is who, which one is slave or God or king,
the blessed deeds bless the smile of help
and always get through
and never strike back."

October 25, 2018

The Poewer of Poetry Perfected

I feel the rivers in your liquid body.
I feel the mountains in your bones.
I am swimming in your river
in your sea and your ocean of silence,
trusting the flow—
You are better, I am convinced.
You are better and even more,
you are closer, I clearly see,
my life being more and more
perfected.

I see the light in your smile.
The light is rolling over,
around and through.
The power of your light
giving the meaning of life.
You are better, I declare,
give this feathered me with no wings, wings,
spread me out against the whitest sky
where the sky's sound is being more and more
perfected.

My heart is unrestrained. My heart is a sun
and my heart is like a wind breathing in

I am going to journey and I am everywhere
I am everything. Breathing out I am loved
by your presence, by your height,
I gift myself to you just like
a poem is gifted
to the closest friends,
and it is my wish, too,
to gift myself to you,

I said I feel you like a river, there is a flow when
I am swimming there is breathe when I am living in
alignment with my wish my truth
I hear you,
I see you are better,
I feel you, I meet you, and more,
and you are more near, and I see you more clearly,
and in my death you are being more
perfected,

Like the silence,
the silence beyond all noise
I am full of mysteries
imperceptibly and immeasurably
I can stay alive and prevail
we are both together, refined and
sowing from here to there,
like a sower casts
seeds on a field,
I eulogize this with praise,

I am an endless body with you — not alone,
shining amongst the nebulas, I am communion
with the divine smile of you
my life is sacred. This is love and expressing it,
especially in the language which lives inside your heart,
is a crown achievement of poetry to me,
because for me poetry itself is a native language of humanity.
The trembling of the morning star, the passage,
between the worlds the door is open,
where the luminous wander in spirit
leaving tracks here, windy, and dusty.

Poetry, which is the answer
to all the mysteries of our world.
Poetry, a reason for the existence of language,
is a breath which brings out every genuine word in
that very moment when I am standing across from myself,
language and poetry itself and have no fear,
because I am free
and now as if you dwell inside me
and as time goes by more and
more, you are near, near to my spirit,
my endless spirit is being more
perfected.

October 18, 2018

Should I Say

Should I say yes, or should I say no?
Should I say maybe, or should I say come on?
Breathe in - breathe out, game over — game starts,
learn how the current moment stands apart

from recent history since the war,
history matters as we know,
what shaped the most contentions
and enduring issue in all of American history?

In all of Georgian history?
In all of the world's history?
And in all of every country's history?
Every tree's and river's history?

Mountain's and sand's history?
Should we say yes, or should we say no,
I only want to know what's going on here
when the moon drips down bedding heavy behind

hearing the wolf's voice who is singing or crying
and the back of the reality's body
all shadowy lined with the imaginary part of noise—
Of silence, with my breath - with my beating heart.

September 6, 2018

You Yourself

Look here friend.
Look with me at this
strange ray.

It is as clean and transparent,
as anything I wanted
to discuss with you
though I've never told you.

Anything I have ever experienced,
but never shared
with you.

You probably become a traveler
when you guess –
You yourself are the space
and you yourself are the time

You become a poet
when you guess—
You yourself are the poetry
and you yourself are the silence

You fall in love
when you guess —

You yourself are the love
and you yourself are the emptiness

You become a warrior
when you guess—
You yourself are the war
and you yourself are the peace

You become a human being
when you guess—
You yourself are the life
and you yourself are God

You give away when you guess—
The whole world is yours
and is for you.

The time passes quickly. Try to guess
and maybe the world will also change.

Why are you here and now... and why do you go there.
Where is heaven... and what can be seen from there.

November 29, 2012

You Are the Center

You are the center—
what's the matter
with you, why are you so sad
why are you so lost,
you are the center of your own living
of your loneliness — of your joy,
the joy with endless dimensions
it never comes unless called,
there is no center of the universe.

There is only the particular universe
of which you are the center.
You are better
when you are giving the shelter
in your heart.
The shelter for whoever needs
the calmness
who needs the comfort.

There is no ideal place where you can
stand idly by while the chatter of mental
illness you are hearing,
while someone else
stands at the center.

You are breath, and you are altar
and where the entire breathe of the universe
comes alive faster and faster.

And more you are silent — more you are audible
You are the reason — you are the focus
of the universe's heart that makes you
possible.

May 21, 2018

You Are Light

Hugging everyone we love—
We glimpse a trace of infinity.
Something inside us remembers the oneness and
this something is breath,
this something is heartbeat,
this something is love itself and himself and herself—
Imagining you are the light.
Yes, my friend, we hunger for eternity.

When you are the light all around you
in every corner and everywhere
and on every side is the light too —
you are everything and everywhere.
Turn to your right and you'll see
and you'll find a shining light.
To your left, splendor — a radiant light.
Yes my friend, we hunger for peace.

Between you and everybody.
Between you and maybe me or someone else.
Because "I am you and what I see is me".
Between them up above, the light of
the presence my friend.

Surrounding that the light of life—
Above it all there is the crown, the crown of light
your love is the crown—

Crowning of aspirations of your own thought,
of your own wish, illuminating the paths of imagination,
spreading the radiance of vision.
This light is unfathomable. Endless.
This light is you and you are brilliant.
But what is this deep need for calmness?
For a personal calmness in a century's
numbness?

You understand — then you lose what you have understood.
The light of that thought suddenly darkens, vanishes,
but then it returns and shines.
You think that you have grasped the light,
when suddenly it escapes, radiating elsewhere.
You pursue it, knowing to catch it.
You cannot bring yourself to die.
You can bring yourself to live

And you keep pursuing it.
That you are — you are the light.
And you are brilliant.
Yes my friend, we hunger for joy.
Build or destroy —there is one choice,

there is no judge — only all planets wheel
if we can touch each other's breath,
if we can feel and make our stand.

August 2, 2018

To Be Written

The old man said to me:
"When I was young, the whole world was young too.
I am old now, but the world remains the same — young."

The old tree said to me:
"When I was young, my mother was
the mother of whole forest
and when I was happy the forest was
happy too and that old man
was a young boy and loved me.
He played underneath me. I am old now, but my mother-tree
remains the same— the mother of whole forest.
She is still young."

The drop of sweat said to me:
"When I was happy, my loved one was happy too,
I am disappearing now, but that old man
and that tree and the sky above,
remain the same and the clouds within
me and the wishes within me
and the sadness within me are not disappearing with me,
and will remain the same."

The old sky said to me:

"I am also old but the grass that covered the valley of summer
is always young and will remain the same."

The old poem said to me:
"I want to be written again.
I want to be written again right in the hearts."

I was listening to them and now I know
the heart of that old man,
the heart of that tree, of that sky above the valley
the heart of that valley also and of course
the heart of that drop of sweat and its loved one
and the heart of everything above or
under or within and in between
or beyond or before, is the heart of us—
this heart is the book of life itself and I want—
as that poem and that man and that tree and that sky
and that valley and that drop of sweat and its loved one
to be written in every single night and every single day
of life, while the writing continues as a breath of us
and that breath remains the same.

August 18, 2018

The World Opens Before Me

The world opens before me, and I see as the words,
as the beams of morning star and celestial bodies
and this is amazingly insufficient for me.

On the palm of my hand the skies are
dropping through the rains,
wishes, yesterday resembles today
and this is amazingly insufficient for me.

You love me, I know, you love me, you always
loved me, always… and with the vision that came as rain,
to be or not to be is insufficient for me.

The time of the universe has ended, my friend…
It is burning you and tearing you
apart… And is calling to itself,
each of us, God.

December 28, 2012

West

Where the West begins is a question that
has puzzled immigrants and
Easterners, they challenge themselves: "What
do I have to give myself…"
Wanting is a state of need. If you know that your own beliefs

Challenge your mind, then you will be the right person…
For right universal time… Where
the West begins is a question
that has puzzled everyone, but

Where the West begins depends on
when you asked the question
the West was anywhere and the West is everywhere
when you are the center of your own

Being, when you are your own center,
the West is a love story, a wonderful, devastating love story
about your illusion and the illusion is a test

and the summer is almost past, the West
is your answer — the West is your question
and your every action is a builder of a future

They attract you like a light in the dark,
the West is the light and at the same time the dark
an internal sign of an awakening inside.

September 1, 2018

The Way Home

As soon as it clears up it becomes dark.
When, like the night, the day sets in.

Impressive.

You'll feel something and guess right away.
That you are being dreamed by yourself.

Impressive and Wonderful.

The pain, as a symbol of life,
will transform into happiness.

Majestic. Everlasting.

As if magic were forgiveness
and that is exactly the way home.

You are immortal, do not forget.

And the way home is exactly the way
to you yourself.

Go ahead…

And the way to you yourself
Is exactly the way to God.

There...

You'll find yourself... You'll find everything there
and you will say — "Hello, I love you."

Yes, you will say — "Hello, I love you."

There, there to you yourself, my friend.
Hello, I love you.

October 23, 2012

Shared Lane

There is a shared lane dear. As we know:
"Who hath ears to hear, let them hear."

As we know: "I wish you were here."
I wish I had been there also

but dear, the Eastern Star is my heart, Milky Way
is my breath and blood in me and thoughts in me,

the thoughts without words, my love.
And our life is a Milky Way—
our life is close to an endless

heart beats, always inside and always
outside and inside out also.
There is a shared lane dear. That's right:

"Who hath ears to hear, let them hear"
the music of your smile, of your calmness, my love

there is a shared lane above,
above the night sky and earth my love.

The shared lane is our breath-touching second to be,
I see you are flying—
I will follow.

Observe the hollow passing up and down
the back and deepening between the days and years, dear,

and centuries and millenniums, my love.
The sound of noise and swallowing is the sound of

history and the present. I see your smile.
I will follow.

August 17, 2018

The Same
Ode to distant friend

Death is the same as life without life.
Evil is the same as kindness without kindness.
Dark is the same as light without light.
Ugliness is the same as beauty without beauty.
Cold is the same as warmth without warmth.
Past is the same as present without present.

Without my friend I am the same as myself without myself.
I feel like I came down to the ground from somewhere above.
Of my feelings above, above my consciousness,
when I saw him, when I recognized him
and as if the sky was left without best friend,
when the star shot from the sky.

Where silence is the same as sound without sound.
Where question is the same as answer without answer.
Where slave is the same as master without freedom.
But what is freedom, my friend? Freedom is love
and love without freedom is not only an illusion,
it's slavery and slavery does not have the same reflection.

"No" is the same as "yes" without "yes"—
we are a reflection

of the future, where future is reflection
of breath, where breath is reflection
of the first idea of being and truth,
but is there a lie that is the same as truth without truth?
Is there something out there without reflections?

The same fable of the wheel—
a wheel is a way
and a way is the reason for destination.
The same meanings.

May 6, 2018

The Light of Wish

There is no way to love, my friend.
Love is the way itself.
Love does not make people.
Love just reveals them… And then

We choose between being right and wrong
and being just kind, just please choose being kind
and you'll be right.
We will fly and run and swim into ourselves
above within — under within and you will have to guess
the meaning of the meaningless.

There is no way to you my love.
You are the way and then
you'll see the light within yourself
the light of your wish
and breath.

July 23, 2018

The Art of E-Art-H

The earth is singing now.
The song is colorful. I always hear this song
and I can sing this song with my heartbeat
and I see this song as a painting.
I can paint it with my heartbeat.
No pain — just calmness.

I can read and write this song as a poem — as a story,
with my breath my heart beats, first.
Earth - the art of silence, the art of presentiment.
Earth - the art of sounds, the art of thirst.
No doubt — just belief.

When I am walking in the dark
and when I am walking in the light
and when I am walking in between
I feel earth as my own twin. Air is my twin
and water is my twin and fire is my twin
and all the languages are my twins in the flesh.

Earth is in silence now — silence is lovely and fresh.
Earth drinks people and plants and stones and oceans
and shadows and birds and stars and nebulas.

It drinks us and our love as a wine to stay alive
in order to forget, in order to
remember.

August 15, 2018

Something Is Important

Maybe we know
something
but not everything
but this something
is more important
than everything.
Because this something
is everything itself
like a breath and the air
and there is no everything
at all
without our wish
to be
in
love.

August 5, 2018

Put Yourself in My Place, Ghost

Put yourself in my place, ghost. Life is short or life is long
we know the circle will come around,
when your mind-mate brings you down

and there's no one, no one else around
but you are still breathing — You don't know why
here's Divine providence — the instinct to be loved,

don't let it get away, a second is like a kiss.
Life is shorter than you think.
Life is longer than you feel.

And you remember yourself, ghost
in the small isolated space where the air was golden
but never penetrated,
nor the smell,
nor the colors,
nor the dust,
nor the heat,
you had a vision of an old time, old books
or even an old man—
his back to the doors, his back to the window wearing a suit
and a hat with a brim like the shadows,
blue shadows,

as the blue wings of a raven,
who spoke about the world—
many years before they were born,
they— your feelings
they— your thoughts.

Put yourself in my place, ghost. Life is short or life is long,
we know the circle will come around, it goes
fast, when your mind-mate brings you down

and from the second we are walking on the planet
we can see the clouds or lakes or suns
with the eyes of sorrow see what's gone
and the second disappeared but the next one will come
and the leaves are dancing all around the fall,
but we're still breathing,
what's done is done.

September 3, 2018

Poetryoga

You have seven keys to the heaven's seven doors,
this second always lives and lilac wind blows

around the second of your shine. The second is now—
now it means again, the moment of breathing, the

moment of being, when winds in your blood are making
their stand when winds in your spirit are making their

shine. All alone or in two's or in three's or even more
on their own after all, stand or fall, the spirits who

really know you and war is already gone from your
mind and you shine. Your moment of being — is the

way of your living. You're breathing, you know the
moment will flow. Universe is floating into your pieces.

You're nebula's ceiling you're nebula's floor and you
shine as you like it and you build as you know.

May 8, 2018

I Hear a Speech, My Love

I hear a speech from deep within.
I see which way the stream flows,
whoever listens to himself will read
the words written with breath and blood,
the breath means the blood.

I realize, much is demanded from me,
but not much is forgiven of me,
I realize, forgiveness is such an enormous thing -
that it can't be only my personal matter,
personal means the forgiveness

and if I realize by what means I want to be special,
then I'll understand who and what I am in reality.
The reality means the wish.
I realize every word is alive and we are alive too,
as long as we understand one another.

As long as we believe in one another,
as long as we are here and then the world
will also survive, the world –
we looked for calm far off and we listened
and that's where we listened,

to the fairytales by Heaven's gate,
to the fairytales on subway walls,
to the fairytales as the key to every secret.
I cannot compare you to anyone in this world
when I reveal to myself how much I love you.

May 5, 2018

I Release You, Go With Peace

You are free from me.
Go wherever you like.
Do whatever you like.
I release you. Go with peace.
May all the mysteries of the universe protect you
and may all the doors open for you. Go.
Years and months, days,
they are giving me the signals, waters also pass.
They change grounds and the calmness
begins to inspire you, go, I release you,
release you with kindness and love,
I love you, you know, involved in yourself

you were presented to me probably by heaven
if I present you with the freedom,
right to remain who you are,
the night will also be cured by the morning,

will be enlightened into various roads,
this final second will now trust in me, too,
as if I am quitting the dream and
the whole bitterness of waking up also
vanishes.

December 9, 2011

I'd like to Explain

I'd like to explain why things fall,
shine or look dull
and planets revolve,
I am searching for my home
in your heart
I am finding the strength
in your smile.

Yes my friend, I am hearing your heart.
Your heartbeat—
the way, I am following music.
Your music of smiling silence.
Your precious calmness of expecting miracles.
The miracles at dawn
and planets revolve.
Your breath is my home.

August 4, 2018

I Transformed

If you know anything about my future,
speak now or forever hold your peace,
and never say anything anywhere, because

I transformed
into a boulder and waited
for someone to appear
as if I had built a city once
and filled the sea with ships through
the crashing waves,

the smoke went beyond the comet sky,
as if I ran to the house of my childhood,
where my childhood was waiting for me intact,
along with the forefeeling of my future
and the stars, the graves of the brothers,
whose fury will be estimated by the time,
when it passes forever and the journey
will be over and the curtains of the universe
will drop, because

I transformed
into the sky and into the jewel of the sky,

I transformed into the blood of Gethsemane,
found the path to lead me,
luckily heard the violet voice today,

then I transformed
into sound and music
and then became the sorrow of dreams
broadcast by satellites,
electronic flowers, roses,

I transformed
into digits, precious stones,
and became the internet's Wi-Fi,
and as a drunk gets drunk in a second,
in a second I circled the clock

and then transformed
into something else again
and that something became a kiss,
how deep is the sky, the universe's edge,
perhaps it is the morning's song?
Between these feelings.

Perhaps I love you? Perhaps I don't?
Perhaps silence has shared its sound with me.
Perhaps poetry has purified me.
I get nervous, you rush to me,

hey, friend, I will remember you.
I will remember you forever and everywhere.
On the both sides of the curtain
the celestial singers,
Divine choristers are taking their places
and the sadness remains, the usual,
heartbreaking, bitter sadness.
No, do not tell me what is awaiting me,
let me be named after the star, because

I transformed.

Time chases me into the falling of waves.
Rivers push along boulders,
and one river will tell me with revelry,
"I will arrive to the coast and wait for you."

The way is long, the way is dusty,
and nobody knows who will meet me,
an enemy or friend, the yin or the yang,
or the orange colors of a distant dawn.
I transformed.

June 8, 2018

If I Can Find You Someone Else Will Find You Too

All your pain will soon be erased.
The sorrow of wondering rapidly gone.
The freedom to praise — the brilliant happening,
searching expecting wonders at dawn.
All the world's mysteries — open them all.

Everything is in you and

if I can find you, someone else will find you too,
someone who, in spite of me, knows where you are,
who is heaven and earth's ally,
feathered with a letter for you to send.

Then be calm when you feel the smell of the rays.
Then be calm when you guess the meaning of noise.
Then be calm when you see the children are playing.
The pain is now gone — the success is coming.
The mind is a playground of the universe's silence.

Everything is in you and

I saw on your website,
that your name was once different,

David Dephy

I'm a labyrinth, a digital vineyard
following the scent of ultraviolet light —

The wind on your head's halo
represented with soft icon lettering.
Look at me, I do not beautify apartments,
tell me if you are who or not

who I found, a ripe star,
a vigilant peck, a drunken smooch
as if the numbers I picked were flowers:
21 - 14 - 24,

A holy trinity, a three-digit code —
to me, three cosmos becoming three jewels,
or the drizzling or snowing when,
opening yourself to me,

You passed by in the distance —
If I can find you, someone else will find you too —
Someone feathered will give you
a letter sealed with heaven and earth's mystery.

January 31, 2018

Naked

Myself said to me:

If it weren't for our spirits, our bodies or even names
if it weren't for our words, our breath or even wishes
we would have been completely naked
after midnight's or morning's mist
after afternoon's or evening's shadows
when our breath began to influence
the universe which is dismissed
in our loneliness under the purple willow tree
there we could see all shapes of time
and shapes of illusions.

I said to myself:

But we already are completely naked
we are in love and we are free
if with a bitter mouth we speak
sweet words and sweetest wishes
the world will not grow wise
or sweet or kind or something else
the world will not grow bitter and it's written
in the book of universe's breath, this book is made by
naked feelings made by life beyond
the death.

August 20, 2018

Our Love Is the Promise

The voice of the heartbeat is the voice of enigma.
The reason for the heartbeat is enigma too… God…
Our love, my sweetest friend is God's
breath from the distance
and the children — our children are
God's thoughts, so proud —
Our love is the promise.

Let's fulfill it — feel free and the children are the songs.
Let's sing them in a loud voice… The voice of enigma…
Our love is also a gift, let's send it as a signal — it will not be
missed, we cannot predict how it will unfold,
Our love is the promise.

Let's share it with the planets and if there is a reason
for them going round and round… And
round and round again
then it's love and only love and love will be found
after centuries of doubt, underneath all enigmas.
Our love is the promise.

August 19, 2018

Please Accept

The lights encircled me.
Please accept.

Sending rays everywhere.
Please accept.

How I wish to show my spirit.
Please accept.

It will calm you and make you happy.
Please accept.

Infinitely transparent.
Please accept.

Infinitely wordy.
Please accept.

Unceasingly vital.
Please accept.

And vitally unceasing.
Please accept.

And rich in lights.
Please accept.

Enriching the colors and the smells of the lights.
Please accept.

Which have always attracted me.
Please accept.

And which are still attracting me.
Please accept.

Lights, lights around us.
Please accept.

I present you their idea.
Please accept.

Unceasingly sincere lights.
Please take them.

Have them as a present from me.
Calmness.

April 16, 2012

For the Sake of Love

If we can ever recognize each other
it is only through love.
Your truth is your bare spirit
and love is your clothing
and your breath,

by changing the world
and unraveling the purpose of life
peace will come upon you,
be in love and millions will be in love,
you will be free and millions will be released.

For the sake of love,
from word to word, from sound to sound,
from color to color, from breath to breath,
from body to body, from time to time,
from man to man, from nation to nation,
from country to country, from plant to plant,
in birds and animals, in fish
and seaweed and
in stones and shells,
trees and insects,
minerals and gems,
stars and nebulas,

galaxies and lights,
my spirit travels and I am always
born and when I fall in love with you
I become free,
from life and death
and I purify
and I am love
God.

May 8, 2018

How Can I

How can I prepare for eternal life,
when life is fleeting…
How can I prepare for death,
when I don't know what it is…
I am listening now…

I am listening to beating now,
the beating of my heart and I see
doubt is deadlier than bullets.
Fear will cut you deeper than knives.
I am listening now…

I am listening to beating now,
the beating of your heart, mother earth
and I see – the tree,
but when I look at a tree,
I see the force,

which makes that tree grow,
with its roots all sunken into the earth,
which raises it up to the sky
and brings it out in flowers.
I am listening now…

I am listening to the beating of your heart, air.
You want to remember it all,
remember every breath around you,
you want to tear out your heart
and give it away with every breath.

Your heart,
always goes to where you love
and where you wish
and how can I not listen to you?
How can I…

How can I prepare for truth,
often you won't be able to tell
the sweet from the bitter
and at times
it's hard to tell them apart.

April 28, 2018

Don't Wait

The present which was the future yesterday
will be the past tomorrow.

Don't wait for a night to fall.
Don't wait for tomorrow's dawn.
Don't even wait for love to come.

Don't wait for any miracle to occur.
Don't wait for loneliness to fade away.
Don't wait for your fate's open arms.
You are happiness.
Yes you are.

Happiness bears your name.
It will find you as a dream does.
Making no distinctions between,
the dust and the stars

Don't wait for anything to finish.
Don't wait for anything to start.
You are the way.
Yes you are.

And whatever is needless
will drop behind
you'll forget them
without bearing a grudge.

Don't wait for your mind to clear up.
Don't wait for the war to stop.
Don't wait for any change to come.
Fall.
Rise.
And fall again
in love.
You are endlessness.
Yes you are.

Fill your heart with joy,
as drops fill oceans,
as if there were nothing and no one
to hurt or kill you.
You are the clue.
Yes you are.

The whole world just is and looks
like what you choose.
The choice is a secret.
And everything
you have ever given away,

will come back through the universe,
to you again.
Don't wait.

October 31, 2011

Deep in the Heart of Heaven

Here is the news—
we have seen what we thought was unseeable,
this is the smile in the dark, the smiling ring of light
surrounding a dark circle deep in the heart of heaven,
deep in the heart of our own expectations, dear friend.
Here is the news—
coming to you every second on the second, wake up.
Event Horizon Telescope like desire of the first kiss,
is calling you, here is the news — here, according to genius'
prophecy, matter, space and time come to an end and vanish
like a dream, like a childhood's fears, we are the children
of heaven, children of that smile in
the dark, this is the journey
from mother earth, as motherhood
is every mother's journey
with her children, wake up. Here is the
news and there is a hope—
the longing for the future, don't ask me what's beyond,
don't say "wake me up when you will see what's beyond,"
because heaven says: "Everything we want
is beyond our fears."

April 12, 2019

I See Your Smile

I see your smile,
when you are leaving home.

I see your smile, when you
are coming back. Thank you.

I can stop and I can feel time,
between these smiles of you.

We can let it go. The path into
the dark is golden. I am moving

forward to reach the point. My
shadow is floating behind me

as the answer of a secret
which had been stolen and we are

hungry for light and still we are
going. Yes, I see your smile.

February 5, 2019

Lord's Verses

I am not worrying now. I've been at peace
with myself and I've been at war with myself,
oh Lord—
I am not worrying now, maybe I've been through
some disappointments and fears, or who knows,
have had some unfair things happen in my life,
I've been at peace with myself and none of that
affects my wish to be myself, none of that affects
my passion which has been put in my silent
delectation by the Lord,
oh Lord—
the gifted poet, an author of the sun, of the universe,
an author of the every verse around me and in my heart.
Sweetness and bitterness, or sweetness of bitterness
they will all steal my freedom—
but only if I let them. But how? If I am in love with myself.
I am a verse of the Lord.
as someone else or no one. My every breath is a letter
and I am writing all my loving, let me do this forever.

May 4, 2019

Oh Lord I See with My Beating Heart

It is due to the fact that we, people do not betray
one another, but ourselves and we betray our vocation.
We betray our ideals and very often we are very well
aware of it... I see with my beating heart...

I see that much is demanded from me, but not much
is forgiven to me... I should respect other people's faults
and opinions as my own ones... I see with my beating heart
poetry is such enormous concept, it can't be only

my personal matter... And if I realize by what means
I want to be special, then I'll understand who and what
I am in reality... Yes, I see with my beating heart
I see—every word is alive and that we are alive too

as long as we understand one another and also that if
in our inner world and in this multi language dictionary
of the mankind survive the words such as Freedom,
then the world will also survive. Yes I see with my

beating heart and for me this is the mission of creations
and of mine as a poet's justification for existence. I am
a verse of the Lord, as someone else or no one.
My every breath is a letter and I am writing

all my loving, let me do this forever.
I only want to know what's going on here
when the moon drips down bedding heavy behind
hearing the wolf's voice who is singing or crying

and the back of the reality's body all shadowy lined
with the imaginary part of noise—of silence,
with my breath—with my beating heart.
Yet, more I am silent—more I am audible.

Yet, I am the reason—I am the focus of the universe's
heart that makes me possible, because I stood on the water,
Yes, I stood on the water in my dream, the bamboo stalk was
swaying, I wish you were with me when the stork flew up.

May 4, 2019

Bear Word to the Spartans

I am listening, owl. Maybe I am dreaming in this silent
twilight, or maybe it's the afternoon now, but it seems
to me I found answers to main questions.

"Stranger, bear word to the Spartans." I am listening, owl.
This is a quote of my first discovery that I am a text and I am
a reader, I am a poet and I am a spirit of solstice king's day.

"Stranger, bear word to the Spartans." I am listening, owl.
It's telling me now that my origins makes me a man, but it
isn't where I came from, absolutely not, it's where I am going,

that counts only, so "Stranger, bear word to the Spartans,"
and say that yes, I found answers to main questions:
Did I sacrifice what I am for what I will be?

Can I say a word and create life? Can I love?
Can I be myself and see the edge of the universe?
I feel—only there, or somewhere, deep in the universe's

heart, there is something tenderly real, tenderly incredible
which waits to be revealed, while I am asking you and
listening, owl: "Stranger, bear word to the Spartans."

May 5, 2019

When I Go Out

When I go out of the New York's subway,
especially through Avenue H by the Q train
in Brooklyn, I hear ocean. Always.
I hear ocean—the sounds of thoughts,
the sounds of wishes and expectations, the sounds of
noise and calmness. I hear solitude.
I hear darkness early in the morning
when I am alone, surrounded only by the sounds as
echoes of my own breath and I am walking faster and
faster and singing, I love a melody as I love the morning.
The morning is a spirit of life for me and a melody is a spirit
of music itself, it is my own breath while I am alive and
can feel the sounds of ocean, as something familiar
is dawning deep within me every morning, then it
disappears again, as I remember my childhood,
the little beetle on my palm and as a kite and valley,
the premonition of joy is forcing me forward,
listening to the melody of breath and looking up to the sky's
wide open silence, the same sky with the same kite from
my childhood, I see we are immortals.

June 14, 2019

The Fireflies

I see the fireflies are rushing to meet the dawn,
I see the tears are rushing to meet the calmness,
the tears always are the words without letters,
and newborn baby always tells the truth without
any word right in mother's heart, right in anyone's
heart, like the rivers also are rushing to meet the sea,
the flood invades my spirit—
I see the tears are becoming the ambassadors of life,
I see the crystal clear ambassadors of future,
when the words are rushing to meet silence
the universe's kiss on our thoughts.

June 18, 2019

Every New Second

The circumstances? No matter what's going on around me,
or inside me, every new second is a chance to reveal
myself in your eyes, in your heart and memories my friend,
without any circumstances.

The circumstances? No matter what's wrong with us,
every new second is a chance to breath, to make love,
the stars are born stars, that's why they grow stars,
without any circumstances.

The circumstances? No matter what are you waiting for,
all we are the stanzas in poetry or paragraphs in prose,
the roses are born roses, that's why they grow roses,
without any circumstances.

The circumstances? No matter what we are, understand
or not, everything is a chance "to be" and don't "or not to be,"
Great men are born great, that's why they grow great,
with or without the circumstances.

June 21, 2019

Acknowledgement

I would like to thank from the bottom of my heart these people: Stephen Frech, Andrea Scrima, Irakli Gabriel, Irakli Todria, Kenneth Kratochvil, Kakha Jelia, Tim Kercher and Julia Melikidze, who have helped me navigate the labyrinths of English language so much.

They generously and unconditionally donated their time so that I could enjoy this special adventure and reach a safe shore without feeling alone. Irakli Gabriel introduced me to the unmatched musicality of the English language, Kenneth Kratochvil showed me what happens to a word when it is spoken in English, Stephen Frech, Tim Kercher, Andrea Scrima, Kakha Jelia and Irakli Todria gave me deeper knowledge of the language and Julia Melikidze taught me patience and opened the door to a world of English verbs.

I am a Georgian/American poet. I understand, it may sound strange, when your native and foreign language meet each other in your consciousness and find a forever home there. But this is love. Yes, love, and expressing it, especially in the language which lives inside your heart, is a crowning achievement of poetry to me, because for me poetry itself is a native language of humanity. Poetry is the answer to all of the mysteries of our unique world. Poetry, a reason for the existence of language, is a breath which brings out every genuine word in that very moment when you are standing across from yourself, language, and poetry itself and have no fear, because you are free. I think that a human being gets strength from the truth and transfers that strength to others and fills them with comfort and allows them to carry on and hold on during everyday struggles. This truth for me is poetry and it has no boundaries. It is timeless and ageless.

DD

About the Author

David Dephy The trilingual Georgian/American poet, novelist, essayist, performer, multimedia artist and painter. The winner of the 2019 Spillwords Press Poetry Award for June's Publication of the Month. His short story "Before The End" was chosen for the *Best European Fiction 2012*, edited by Aleksandar Hemon and prefaced by Nicole Krauss, and published in the U.S. by Dalkey Archive Press.

An active participant in the American and international poetry and artistic scenes, such as PEN World Voices, 92Y Poetry Center, Voices of Poetry, Long Island Poetry Listings, New

York Public Library, Starr Bar Poetry Series, Columbia University – School of the Arts in the City of New York, Bowery Poetry Club which named him a Literature Luminary.

He was an artist-in-residence at the writer's residency Ledig House in Ghent, New York and a participate in the PEN World Voices festival in New York City, where he presented a live poetry event entitled "The Second Skin" with Laurie Anderson, Yusef Komunyakaa and Salman Rushdie at the Unterberg Poetry Center, 92nd Str Y.

He performed a live poetry show with quadraphonic audio system at the Abastumani's Observatory of Georgia and was chosen as an Ambassador of Poetry by Austrian worldwide brand Julius Meinl in Georgia.

David Dephy's poetry /live performance The Poet King and The Easter Verses at the Peace Cathedral of the Evangelical Baptist Church of Georgia included in the Divine Liturgies officially.

His poetry has been published and anthologized in USA and all over the world by the many literary magazines. He lives and works in New York City.

PUBLISHING CREDITS:

Eastern Star – Adelaide Magazine, USA

The Path into the Dark is Golden – Best Poetry Magazine, USA **Politics is the Art of Choices** – Dissident Voice, USA

If I Can Find You Someone Else Will Find You Too – Oddball Magazine, USA

People – Vistitant Magazine, USA

The Sea is So Calm Now – Statorec Magazine, USA

The Interpretation – Poetica Review, USA / UK

The Fireflies – Spillwords Press, USA – *The Night of Kiss* Anthologized by Culture Cult Magazine, / *The Summer's Night* published by Academy of the Heart and Mind, USA

When I Go Out – Academy of the Heart and Mind, USA

Deep in the Heart of Heaven – Spillwords Press Magazine as a feature poem, USA

The Art of the E-Art-h – Apricity Magazine by the University of Texas in Austin, USA

In Front of the Mirror – Spillwords Press, USA

www.ingramcontent.com/pod-product-compliance
Lightning Source LLC
Chambersburg PA
CBHW032237080426
42735CB00008B/892